A Leader without a Position

Paulette Durand

Paulette Durand

Paulette Durand

Paulette Durand

Index

Lead Ourselves

Leading ourselves is the first step on the path to true leadership. Before thinking about leading other people, it is essential that we learn to be leaders of our own lives. This idea may sound simple, but in reality, it is one of the biggest challenges we face. Leading our lives means taking control of our decisions, being responsible for our actions and, above all, being aware of our own being. It is a process that involves knowing ourselves on a deep level, understanding our motivations, values, and what drives us to act.

By leading ourselves, we begin to build a solid foundation upon which we can develop our leadership capabilities with others. This self-leadership is not simply making decisions on our own, but making decisions that are aligned with our principles and values. It is being able to look in the mirror and be proud of the person we are seeing, not for what we have achieved in external terms, but for the way we have managed our lives. This type of leadership is what helps us stay firm in our convictions, even when we face pressure or temptation to act against what we know is right.

To lead ourselves, we first need to develop deep self-awareness. This means being in tune with our thoughts, emotions, and behaviors. It is a continuous process of reflection and self-evaluation. We ask ourselves why we do what we do, what motivates us, and how our actions affect both ourselves and those around us. This introspection is vital because, without it, we run the risk of acting impulsively or being easily influenced by external factors, losing sight of what really matters to us.

In addition to self-awareness, personal leadership requires a strong dose of self-discipline. Leading ourselves means being able to do what is necessary, even when it is not easy. It means setting clear goals and working toward them, despite the challenges and distractions that may arise. Self-discipline is what allows us to stay focused and committed to our goals, even in times when motivation may falter. It's what drives us to keep going when things get tough and to stay on the right path.

Another crucial aspect of personal leadership is responsibility. When we lead our lives, we accept full responsibility for our actions and decisions. We do not blame others for our failures nor do we expect others to solve our problems. Instead, we recognize that we are the architects of our own lives and that our choices determine our destiny. This mindset empowers us, because we realize that we have the power to change our situation if we are not satisfied with it. By accepting full responsibility for our lives, we free ourselves from the victim mentality and take control of our future.

Leading ourselves also means being aware of our limitations and being willing to continually improve. None of us are perfect, and there will always be areas where we can grow. A good personal leader is someone who not only recognizes his or her weaknesses but also takes active steps to overcome them. This could mean seeking to learn new skills, working on our emotional intelligence, or simply being more patient and understanding with ourselves and others. Personal leadership is a constant journey of improvement, in which every day we strive to be a better version of ourselves.

Finally, leading ourselves requires having a clear vision of what we want to achieve in life. This vision acts as our compass, guiding us in our daily decisions and actions. Without a clear vision, it is easy to get lost in the chaos of everyday life, reacting to circumstances rather than acting proactively. A personal vision gives us direction and purpose, helps us prioritize what is truly important, and keeps us motivated on our path to success. By staying focused on our vision, we can lead our lives with intention and determination.

In short, leading ourselves is a comprehensive process that encompasses self-awareness, self-discipline, accountability, continuous improvement, and having a clear vision. It is the foundation on which everything else in leadership is built. Without this solid foundation, any attempt to lead others will be fragile and possibly unsustainable. By becoming the leaders of our own lives, we not only prepare ourselves to lead others, but we also ensure that we live a life that is full, meaningful, and in tune with our deepest values. It is a path that requires effort and commitment, but the rewards are incalculable.

The Foundation of Leadership

The basis of leadership is self-knowledge, a concept that may seem abstract or complicated, but is actually quite simple: it is about knowing ourselves deeply and honestly. To be a good leader, we must first understand who we are, what motivates us, what our core values are, and how our experiences and emotions influence our decisions and behaviors. Without this knowledge, any leadership we attempt to exercise will be superficial and lack authenticity. It's like building a house without a foundation; Sooner or later, it will collapse.

Self-knowledge begins with reflection. We need to take time to think about ourselves, something that is often overlooked in everyday life. What are our strengths? What are our weaknesses? What are we really passionate about? These are important questions that we should ask ourselves regularly. By answering them, we begin to form a clearer picture of who we are and what drives us. This image is not something static; It changes over time as we grow and learn. Therefore, self-knowledge is a continuous process that requires our constant attention.

Part of self-knowledge also involves accepting our imperfections. We all have aspects of our personality or behavior that we would prefer not to have. Maybe we are impatient, or maybe we have a hard time delegating tasks because we feel like no one else can do them as well as we can. Whatever the case, recognizing these weaknesses is essential. It's not about judging ourselves harshly, but about being honest with ourselves. Once we recognize our areas of improvement, we can work on them and by doing so, we strengthen our ability to lead. Ignoring our weaknesses or pretending they don't exist will only lead to bigger problems in the future.

Another key aspect of self-knowledge is understanding our core values. Values are those principles or beliefs that we consider most important in life. They can include things like honesty, fairness, compassion, or responsibility. Our values guide our decisions and actions, whether we are aware of it or not. When we lead from a place of alignment with our values, our actions are more consistent and authentic, making us more effective and respected as leaders. However, to lead from our values, we must first identify what they are. This requires honest introspection and sometimes a re-evaluation of what really matters to us.

Self-knowledge also includes understanding our motivations. Why do we do what we do? What drives us to get up every day and face life's challenges? Some people are motivated by the desire to help others, while others may be driven by the search for personal achievement or recognition. Whatever our motivation, it is important to be aware of it, because our motivations influence how we lead. A leader who is motivated primarily by the desire to serve others will likely make different decisions than a leader who is more focused on personal success. No motivation is necessarily better than another, but knowing ours allows us to lead more consciously and deliberately.

In addition to our strengths, weaknesses, values and motivations, self-knowledge also involves understanding how our past experiences have shaped us. We have all gone through moments of success and failure, happiness and pain. These experiences have left their mark on us and have influenced the person we are today. By reflecting on our experiences, we can learn valuable lessons that help us grow as leaders. For example, a past failure may have taught us the importance of perseverance, while a success may have shown us the value of preparation and effort. By connecting our past experiences with our current leadership, we can lead with more wisdom and perspective.

It is important to highlight that self-knowledge is not a destination that is reached, but rather a continuous journey. As we move through life, we continue to learn about ourselves, discovering new facets of our personalities, and adjusting our leadership approach accordingly. This constant learning process is what allows us to evolve as leaders and adapt to the changes and challenges we face. We should not be afraid to change or reevaluate our beliefs and values as we gain new experiences and knowledge. In fact, the willingness to change is a sign of a truly strong and confident leader.

In conclusion, the basis of leadership is self-knowledge. Without a deep understanding of who we are, our strengths and weaknesses, our values and motivations, we cannot lead effectively. This self-knowledge provides us with the solid foundation upon which we can build our leadership skills, allowing us to lead with authenticity, consistency and purpose. By embarking on the journey of self-knowledge, we not only prepare ourselves to be better leaders, but we also enrich our personal lives, making our interactions with others more meaningful and our decisions more aligned with who we are at our core.

The Power of Self-Efficacy

The power of self-efficacy is one of the most important aspects of personal leadership, and refers to the belief we have in our ability to face and overcome the challenges presented to us. When we talk about self-efficacy, we are referring to that internal voice that tells us that we are capable of achieving what we set out to do, that we can learn new skills, adapt to difficult situations and overcome obstacles. This belief is not simply a matter of self-confidence; It is a deep conviction that, with effort and perseverance, we can succeed in our goals and aspirations.

Self-efficacy is critical to leadership because, without it, it is easy to fall into hopelessness or inaction when faced with challenges. Imagine someone who constantly doubts their ability to handle difficult situations. Whenever a problem arises, that person may feel overwhelmed, doubt his or her abilities, and as a result, may avoid making important decisions or delegate those decisions to others. This lack of self-efficacy not only impacts your ability to lead others, but also limits your personal and professional growth. In contrast, a person with a strong sense of self-efficacy will approach challenges with a positive attitude, trusting that even though things are difficult, he has the ability to solve them.

Self-efficacy is not something we are born with; It is something that develops over time, through our experiences and the way we interpret those experiences. One of the most important factors that influences our self-efficacy is previous success. When we achieve something we set out to do, especially if it was difficult, our self-efficacy is strengthened. This success reinforces the belief that we are capable of facing and overcoming similar challenges in the future. For example, if we have overcome a significant obstacle at work or in our personal life, we are more likely to believe in our ability to overcome other challenges in the future.

However, self-efficacy is not built on success alone. It is also strengthened when we learn from our failures. Although no one likes to fail, the way we handle failure can have a profound impact on our self-efficacy. If we interpret failure as an opportunity to learn and grow, rather than seeing it as proof of our limitations, we can emerge stronger and with greater confidence in our abilities. This process of learning from adversity is what transforms failures into valuable lessons that fuel our self-efficacy.

Another crucial aspect of self-efficacy is the influence of the people around us. People who support and encourage us can have a big impact on how we perceive our own abilities. When someone we trust tells us that they believe in us, that we are capable of achieving our goals, this can reinforce our own belief in ourselves. On the other hand, if we are surrounded by people who doubt our abilities or constantly criticize us, this can weaken our self-efficacy. For this reason, it is important to surround ourselves with people who support us and help us see our strengths, especially in times of doubt.

Self-efficacy is also related to our ability to set goals and work toward them. When we believe in our ability to succeed, we are more willing to set ambitious goals and work hard to achieve them. This willingness to challenge oneself and push ourselves beyond what we think is possible is what allows us to grow as leaders and as people. On the other hand, if we doubt our abilities, we are likely to avoid setting challenging goals or give up easily when things get difficult. This type of mindset limits our potential and prevents us from achieving our most important goals.

A factor that also strengthens self-efficacy is modeling, that is, observing other people who have been successful in challenges similar to ours. When we see someone we admire achieving something significant, it gives us an example of what is possible. It shows us that, with effort and determination, we can also achieve success. Modeling is especially powerful when the person we observe has similar characteristics or circumstances to our own, as this allows us to more easily identify with their achievements and feel that we can do it too.

It is important to understand that self-efficacy does not mean that we should always feel confident in our abilities or that we should never have doubts. We all face times of uncertainty and challenge. The key is how we respond to those moments. A person with a strong sense of self-efficacy is not someone who never doubts, but rather someone who, despite doubts, moves forward, trusts in his ability to find a solution, and does not give up at the first sign of difficulty. It is that perseverance and self-confidence that defines a strong leader.

In short, the power of self-efficacy lies in the deep belief in our ability to face and overcome life's challenges. It is an internal force that drives us to act, to learn from our mistakes and to move forward, even when things get difficult. Self-efficacy is developed through our experiences, both success and failure, and is reinforced by the support of the people around us and by the examples of those who have achieved success before us. By strengthening our self-efficacy, we prepare ourselves to face any challenge that comes our way and to lead with confidence and determination. This inner power is what allows us to not only survive, but thrive, and is one of the most important foundations of effective leadership.

Lead with Emotional Intelligence

Leading with emotional intelligence is an essential skill in modern leadership, and refers to the ability to understand, manage and use our emotions effectively to make decisions, solve problems and relate to others. Emotional intelligence is not just an abstract concept, it is a practical skill that can significantly improve our ability to lead, not only others, but also ourselves. By developing this skill, we become more aware of how our emotions influence our actions and the actions of those around us, allowing us to lead with greater empathy, clarity, and effectiveness.

Emotional intelligence begins with self-awareness, which is the ability to recognize our own emotions as they arise. Emotions can often be automatic reactions and, if we are not aware of them, they can influence our behavior without us realizing it. For example, if we are frustrated or angry, we might react impulsively, saying or doing things we will later regret. By developing self-awareness, we learn to identify these emotions in the moment, which gives us the opportunity to manage our responses in a more controlled and deliberate way. This awareness not only helps us avoid impulsive mistakes, but also allows us to lead with a calmer and more rational approach.

In addition to self-awareness, emotional intelligence also includes self-regulation, which is the ability to manage our emotions constructively. We all experience strong emotions from time to time, whether it's stress, anger, or sadness, but the key is how we handle them. Self-regulation involves taking a moment to reflect before reacting, allowing us to choose a more appropriate and less impulsive response. This is especially important in leadership, where our decisions and actions can have a great impact on others. A leader who is capable of self-regulation is someone who can remain calm in difficult situations, make thoughtful decisions, and maintain a positive and productive work environment.

Empathy is another crucial component of emotional intelligence. Empathy means being able to put yourself in the shoes of others, understand their emotions and perspectives, and respond in a compassionate and respectful way. In the context of leadership, empathy allows us to better connect with the people we lead, understand their needs and concerns, and support them more effectively. An empathetic leader is able to build stronger, more meaningful relationships, which in turn fosters an environment of trust and collaboration. Empathy not only improves our interpersonal relationships, but also helps us make more fair and equitable decisions, considering the impact of our actions on others.

Emotional intelligence also extends to our communication skills. An emotionally intelligent leader is someone who can communicate his thoughts and emotions clearly, openly and honestly, without being dominated by her emotions. This means being able to express our ideas and feelings in a way that others can understand and respond positively, avoiding misunderstandings and conflicts. In addition, effective communication also involves being a good listener, paying attention to the emotions and needs of others. By developing our emotional communication skills, we not only improve our ability to lead, but we also foster a work environment where people feel heard and valued.

Relationship management is another fundamental aspect of emotional intelligence in leadership. Interpersonal relationships are a crucial part of leadership, and how we manage these relationships can determine our success or failure as leaders. Emotional intelligence helps us build and maintain positive relationships, based on trust and mutual respect. It allows us to resolve conflicts constructively, negotiate with empathy and find solutions that benefit all parties involved. A leader who manages their relationships well is someone who can bring people together, inspire them to work together toward a common goal, and create a harmonious and productive work environment.

Another important aspect of leading with emotional intelligence is motivation, both our own motivation and the ability to motivate others. Emotional intelligence helps us stay motivated, even in difficult situations, by connecting our emotions with our goals and values. It allows us to maintain a positive and resilient attitude, even when facing challenges, which in turn inspires others to keep going. Additionally, an emotionally intelligent leader is someone who can motivate their team, recognizing and appreciating their efforts, and helping them see meaning and purpose in their work. Emotional motivation not only drives our performance, but also fosters a sense of commitment and satisfaction in those around us.

It is important to note that emotional intelligence is not an innate ability that only a few possess; It is something that we can all develop and improve over time. By practicing self-awareness, self-regulation, empathy, effective communication, relationship management, and motivation, we can strengthen our emotional intelligence and become more effective leaders. This process takes time and effort, but the rewards are immense. It not only makes us better leaders, but also better people, able to manage our emotions in healthy ways, connect with others more deeply, and navigate life's challenges with greater resilience and grace.

In conclusion, leading with emotional intelligence is essential to being an effective leader in today's world. It allows us to understand and manage our own emotions, as well as those of others, so that we can make informed decisions, solve problems and build strong, positive relationships. By developing our emotional intelligence, we prepare ourselves to face the challenges of leadership with a clear mind and a compassionate heart, which not only benefits us, but also the people we lead. This approach not only helps us be more effective leaders, but also creates an environment in which everyone can thrive, contributing to collective success and overall well-being.

The Key to Leadership

The key to leadership, what truly distinguishes an effective leader from others, is not technical skill or specialized knowledge. The key to leadership is the ability to influence others positively, inspire them to be the best they can be, and guide a group toward achieving common goals with a shared sense of purpose and direction. This influence is not based on the authority or power that a leader may have over others, but on the trust, respect and connection that a leader is able to establish with the people around them.

To understand this key, it is essential to recognize that leadership is not simply a matter of giving orders or being the smartest person in the room. Leading is not just about having the last word, but about being a facilitator, someone who helps others reach their full potential. This ability to influence and guide others is based on authenticity. An authentic leader is someone who acts in accordance with his or her values and principles, and who is genuine in his or her interactions with others. This authenticity builds trust, and trust is the foundation on which strong and effective relationships are built in any group or organization.

Trust is an essential element of leadership, and it is earned through consistency between what we say and what we do. When our actions are aligned with our words, people begin to trust us. This consistency not only reinforces our credibility as leaders, but also sets a standard for others. A leader who acts with integrity and consistency inspires others to do the same, creating an environment in which everyone feels valued and respected. Trust is not built overnight; It is the result of a constant effort to be honest and transparent in all our interactions.

Another key aspect of leadership is the ability to inspire others. Inspiring is not simply motivating people to do something; is to help them see a greater purpose in what they do, to find meaning in their work that goes beyond everyday tasks. An inspirational leader is someone who can articulate a clear and compelling vision for the future, and who can communicate that vision in a way that resonates with the aspirations and values of others. When people feel inspired, they are more willing to commit, work harder, and overcome challenges, because they see that their efforts contribute to something bigger than themselves.

The ability to communicate effectively is another fundamental key to leadership. A leader must be able to express his or her ideas and expectations in a clear and understandable manner, and must also be a good listener. Listening is as important as speaking, because it is through listening that a leader can understand the needs, concerns and perspectives of others. Effective communication is not just about transmitting information, but creating a dialogue in which everyone feels heard and valued. This ability to communicate and listen effectively strengthens relationships and fosters an environment of collaboration and mutual support.

In addition to communication and inspiration, empathy is an essential quality in leadership. Empathy allows a leader to understand and connect with the emotions and experiences of others. An empathetic leader not only cares about results, but also about the well-being of the people who are part of the team. This genuine concern for others creates a work environment where people feel supported and understood, which in turn improves morale and motivation. Empathy also helps a leader make more informed and fair decisions by considering how those decisions will affect others.

Leadership also involves the ability to make difficult decisions and take responsibility for those decisions. An effective leader does not shy away from difficult decisions, but faces them with courage and determination. However, making decisions does not mean acting in an authoritarian manner or without consulting others. A good leader involves his team in the decision-making process, seeks different perspectives, and is willing to reconsider his position if necessary. This collaborative approach not only improves the quality of decisions, but also strengthens the sense of belonging and commitment within the team.

Resilience is another essential component of the key to leadership. Being a leader means facing challenges, setbacks and moments of uncertainty. Resilience is the ability to bounce back from those challenges, to learn from failures, and to move forward with renewed energy and determination. A resilient leader is someone who does not crumble in the face of adversity, but instead finds a way to adapt and guide their team through difficult times. This resilience is not only important for the leader's survival, but also serves as an example to others, showing that it is possible to overcome any obstacle with the right attitude and approach.

Finally, the key to leadership includes the ability to foster the development of others. A leader is not someone who cares only about his or her own success, but someone who is dedicated to helping others grow and reach their full potential. This means providing opportunities for learning and development, offering constructive feedback and supporting people on their journey of personal and professional growth. A leader who invests in the development of his team creates an environment in which everyone feels empowered and motivated to contribute to collective success.

In short, the key to leadership is not found in power or authority, but in the ability to positively influence, inspire and guide others, and build relationships based on trust, communication and empathy. It is an ongoing process that requires self-awareness, integrity, and a genuine commitment to the well-being and development of others. Leading successfully means facing challenges with resilience, making difficult decisions with courage, and always being willing to learn and grow together with the team. This is the essence of leadership, and it is what truly defines an effective and respected leader. By understanding and applying these keys in our lives, we not only become better leaders, but we also contribute to creating a world where everyone can thrive and reach their full potential.

Leadership from Empathy

Leading from empathy is an approach that transforms traditional leadership into a more human and connected experience. Empathy, at its core, is the ability to put yourself in the shoes of others, to understand and feel what other people are experiencing. It's not just about sympathizing with someone, but really understanding their emotions, perspectives, and circumstances. This type of leadership not only improves relationships within a team, but also creates a work environment where people feel valued, understood and supported, which in turn increases motivation, collaboration and commitment of all employees. involved.

When we talk about empathetic leadership, we are referring to an approach in which the leader sincerely cares about the well-being of others. This means that the leader not only focuses on results and meeting goals, but also takes into account how the people under his guidance feel. Understanding the emotions of others is not an easy task, but it is crucial to creating a healthy and productive work environment. An empathetic leader is one who takes the time to actively listen, observe, and be present in interactions with his or her team. This willingness to truly understand people is what separates an empathetic leader from one who only focuses on numbers.

One of the first steps to leading with empathy is to develop the skill of listening carefully. Listening not only involves hearing the words someone says, but also picking up on tone, facial expression, and body language. Many times, people do not directly express what they feel, either because of fear, insecurity, or because they do not know how to do so. An empathetic leader pays attention to these non-verbal cues and seeks to understand what is really going on in the minds and hearts of others. By actively listening, a leader shows respect for the person who is speaking, which in turn strengthens trust and the relationship between the two.

In addition to active listening, empathy in leadership also involves the ability to offer emotional support. This means being available to others in times of difficulty, whether personal or professional. An empathetic leader does not limit himself to giving orders or expecting results; He is also there to offer comfort, advice, or simply be a calming presence when someone needs it. This type of support can make a big difference in how a person handles stress, pressure, or difficult situations. Knowing that they have someone to rely on can help people overcome challenges with greater confidence and resilience.

Empathy is also reflected in decision making. An empathetic leader considers the impact of his decisions not only on the final results, but also on the people involved. Before making an important decision, an empathetic leader asks themselves how it will affect each team member, how they will feel, and what emotional repercussions it might have. This type of consideration does not mean that a leader should avoid difficult decisions, but rather that they should approach them with sensitivity and understanding, always looking for ways to minimize the negative impact on others. This perspective helps build a work environment where people feel respected and valued, even in difficult situations.

Another dimension of empathetic leadership is the ability to recognize and celebrate the achievements of others. An empathetic leader understands that recognition and appreciation are fundamental to people's motivation and well-being. When a team member accomplishes something important, the leader takes the time to recognize that achievement, to express gratitude, and to make the person feel valued. This recognition doesn't have to be grandiose or public; Sometimes a simple word of thanks or a gesture of personal recognition can have a profound impact. By genuinely showing appreciation, a leader strengthens the relationship with her team and fosters a positive and encouraging work environment.

Leadership from empathy also implies being flexible and adaptive in managing interpersonal relationships. Each person is different, with their own personality, background and ways of seeing the world. An empathetic leader recognizes these differences and adjusts his or her approach according to the needs and characteristics of each individual. This could mean adapting communication style, offering different types of support, or adjusting expectations to better align with each person's capabilities and circumstances. This flexibility not only makes the team function more harmoniously, but also demonstrates that the leader values each person as a unique individual, not just a resource or part of the team.

Leading from empathy also has a significant impact on organizational culture. A leader who practices empathy sets a tone for the entire organization, creating an environment where compassion, understanding, and mutual respect are core values. This empathetic culture not only improves employee satisfaction and well-being, but can also lead to greater talent retention, better cross-departmental collaboration, and greater innovation. When people feel safe and supported, they are more willing to share ideas, take calculated risks, and contribute more meaningfully to the organization's success.

It is important to note that empathy should not be seen as a weakness or something that compromises a leader's authority. In fact, empathy strengthens leadership by building a solid foundation of trust and respect. An empathetic leader is not someone who avoids conflict or deviates from goals to please everyone; He is someone who faces challenges with a deep understanding of human emotions and needs. This understanding allows the leader to make more informed decisions, build more cohesive teams, and achieve results more effectively and sustainably.

In short, leading with empathy is an approach that puts people at the center of leadership. It is about understanding and connecting with others on an emotional level, actively listening, offering support, making decisions considering the impact on people, and recognizing and celebrating individual and collective achievements. Empathy in leadership not only improves interpersonal relationships, but also creates a work environment where everyone feels valued, understood, and motivated to do their best. This approach not only makes the leader more effective, but also contributes to a more humane, more cohesive, and ultimately more successful organization.

The Language of Leadership

The language of leadership is a powerful tool that goes beyond the words we use in our daily interactions. It is the way we communicate, both verbally and non-verbally, and it is one of the main ways leaders can influence, motivate and inspire others. The language of leadership is not just about what is said, but also how it is said. It includes tone of voice, word choice, body language, and the ability to listen and respond effectively. A leader who masters this language can connect more deeply with people, convey their vision clearly, and guide their team to success.

One of the first things we must understand about the language of leadership is that every word counts. The words we choose can have a lasting impact on those around us. A leader aware of this selects his words carefully, making sure they are clear, positive and action-oriented. For example, instead of saying "this is a problem," a leader could say "this is an opportunity to improve." Changing perspective through language can change the way people perceive a situation, making them feel more empowered and optimistic. This positive approach not only encourages a more proactive mindset, but also helps keep morale high on the team, even during difficult times.

Tone of voice is another crucial aspect of leadership language. It's not just what we say, but how we say it, that can make the difference. A warm, encouraging tone of voice can make people feel valued and respected, while a cold or authoritarian tone can create distance and resentment. Effective leaders are aware of how their tone of voice affects others and adjust it according to the situation. In times of stress or tension, a calm, confident tone can help put others at ease and maintain a clear focus on problem-solving. In situations where an achievement is celebrated, a tone of enthusiasm and joy can increase motivation and strengthen the sense of team.

Body language is also an integral part of leadership language. Often, what is not said in words is communicated through the body. A leader who maintains an open and relaxed posture, makes eye contact, and is receptive to others sends a message of trust and approachability. On the other hand, crossing your arms, avoiding eye contact, or having a tense posture can give the impression of being closed off or disinterested. It is important for leaders to be aware of their body language and use it to reinforce their verbal message. Good nonverbal communication can strengthen trust between the leader and his or her team, creating an environment in which people feel comfortable expressing their ideas and concerns.

Active listening is another essential component of leadership language. Listening is not simply hearing what someone says; It is being present in the conversation, grasping the meaning behind the words, and responding in a way that demonstrates understanding and consideration. A leader who practices active listening makes people feel valued and respected. This skill also allows the leader to better understand the needs and perspectives of their team, which can lead to more informed decisions and more effective solutions. Additionally, active listening strengthens the relationship between the leader and others, fostering an environment of trust and collaboration.

The language of leadership also includes the ability to ask effective questions. Well-posed questions can open new perspectives, challenge assumptions, and encourage critical thinking. A leader who asks questions not only seeks to obtain information, but also to stimulate reflection and growth in others. For example, instead of giving a direct solution to a problem, a leader might ask, "What options have you considered?" or "How could we approach this differently?" These questions not only involve others in the decision-making process, but also encourage them to develop their own problem-solving skills and think more creatively.

Empathy is another important dimension of leadership language. An empathetic leader uses language that recognizes and validates the emotions of others. This could be as simple as saying, "I understand this must be difficult for you" or "I appreciate how you feel about this." By acknowledging the emotions of others, a leader shows that he cares about people, not just results. This approach not only improves the relationship between the leader and his or her team, but also creates an environment where people feel safe to be honest and open about their challenges and concerns. Empathy in the language of leadership not only facilitates better communication, but also strengthens the sense of community and mutual support.

Consistency between verbal and non-verbal language is essential in leadership. A leader's words must be aligned with his actions and body language. If a leader says he values his team's ideas, but then doesn't pay attention when someone shares an idea, there's a disconnect that can undermine trust and respect. Consistency reinforces the leader's credibility and ensures that his message is received the way he intended. When words and actions are aligned, the leader projects authenticity and trustworthiness, which strengthens the influence and impact he or she has on others.

Another facet of leadership language is the ability to inspire through communication. An inspiring leader is able to articulate a clear and compelling vision of the future, so that others are motivated to follow that vision. This involves not only describing a goal, but also connecting that goal to people's values and aspirations. By doing so, a leader can transform a mundane task into a meaningful mission, increasing team commitment and dedication. Inspiration through language is not just about using big words, but about connecting emotionally with others so that they feel that their work has real purpose and impact.

The language of leadership also involves the ability to give feedback constructively. Feedback is a crucial part of development and continuous improvement, but it must be handled carefully to be effective. A leader who gives feedback constructively focuses on the behaviors and results, not the person, and offers clear suggestions for improvement. For example, instead of saying, "This was not good," a leader could say, "In this situation, you could have considered this alternative to obtain a better outcome." This approach not only helps the person understand how they can improve, but also prevents them from feeling attacked or demoralized. Constructive feedback is a powerful tool for growth, both individual and organizational.

Finally, the language of leadership includes the ability to create a sense of belonging and community. A leader who uses inclusive and collaborative language fosters an environment in which everyone feels part of a team. This could be as simple as using "we" instead of "I" or "you," reinforcing the idea that everyone is working together toward a common goal. Language that promotes inclusion and collaboration not only strengthens team cohesion, but also ensures that everyone feels valued and respected for their contribution.

In short, the language of leadership is much more than the words you choose; It is a combination of verbal and non-verbal communication, active listening, effective questioning, empathy, consistency, inspiration, constructive feedback, and a focus on inclusion and collaboration. A leader who masters this language can influence more effectively, connect more deeply with his team, and guide his organization to success. By understanding and applying the principles of leadership language, we not only become better communicators, but also more effective leaders, able to inspire, motivate, and guide others to meaningful and lasting achievements.

Building Trust Relationships

Building trusting relationships is one of the cornerstones of effective leadership. Trust is the foundation on which any strong relationship is based, whether in a professional, personal or community setting. In the context of leadership, trust is what allows a team to function harmoniously, for people to feel safe to share their ideas and concerns, and for progress toward common goals with cohesion and commitment. Without trust, it is almost impossible for a leader to guide his team effectively, as distrust breeds uncertainty, fear and lack of commitment.

Trust is not granted automatically; it must be earned and built over time. For a leader, this means acting consistently, being honest and transparent, and demonstrating integrity in every action. People trust leaders who keep their promises, who act on what they say, and who make decisions with integrity. This type of consistency between words and actions is crucial, as any discrepancy can quickly undermine the trust a leader has worked to build. When team members see that a leader acts with integrity, they are more willing to trust them, which facilitates open communication and effective collaboration.

Transparency is another key element in building trust. A transparent leader is one who shares information openly and honestly, without hiding important details or making decisions behind closed doors. Transparency doesn't mean sharing absolutely everything, but it does mean that a leader clearly explains the reasons behind their decisions, is open about the challenges the team faces, and is willing to admit when they don't have all the answers. This openness creates an environment in which people feel informed and involved in what is happening, which in turn reinforces trust. When people feel that they have the necessary information and that nothing is hidden from them, they are more willing to trust the leader's decisions and support the leader's vision.

Active listening is also essential to building trusting relationships. A listening leader not only hears the words, but also grasps the meaning and emotions behind what is said. Active listening shows others that their opinions are valued and that their concerns are important. When a leader listens genuinely, he sets a tone of mutual respect, which strengthens the relationship between the leader and team members. This type of listening is not just limited to in-person conversations; It is also reflected in the leader's ability to be available and accessible, whether in meetings, by email or in other communication channels. Accessibility and willingness to listen reinforce trust, as people know they can come to their leader with any issue, big or small.

Empathy is another powerful tool in building trust. An empathetic leader is one who can put themselves in the shoes of others, understand their emotions and perspectives, and act according to that understanding. Empathy not only helps leaders connect on a deeper level with their team members, but it also facilitates conflict resolution and decision-making that considers the well-being of everyone involved. When people feel that their leader truly cares about them, they are more willing to trust them, be honest, and fully commit to teamwork. Empathy is not just about being kind; It is a skill that builds confidence by showing others that their feelings and experiences are understood and valued.

In addition to empathy, building trusting relationships also requires consistency in the leader's behavior. People trust those who are predictable in their actions and responses. This means that a leader must be consistent in how he treats people, how he makes decisions, and how he handles challenges. Consistency creates a sense of security and predictability, allowing people to feel more comfortable and confident in their work environment. If a leader is inconsistent or unpredictable, trust can quickly erode as people will not know what to expect or how to behave to maintain a positive relationship with the leader.

Building trusting relationships also involves giving trust to others. A leader who trusts his team, who delegates responsibilities and who believes in people's capabilities, is laying the foundation for a relationship based on mutual trust. When a leader shows confidence in her team, team members feel valued and motivated to meet expectations.

This trust must be genuine, not just an act of empty words. It involves allowing people to make decisions, make mistakes and learn from them, without fear of being punished. This type of environment encourages innovation and growth, as people feel safe to try new ideas and take calculated risks.

Another important aspect in building trust is the leader's ability to fairly and equitably handle conflicts and disagreements. In any group, differences of opinion will arise, and the way a leader handles these situations can strengthen or weaken trust. A leader who approaches conflict impartially, who listens to all parties involved, and who seeks solutions that benefit everyone, is demonstrating that he values justice and mutual respect. This approach not only resolves conflicts effectively, but also reinforces confidence in the leader's ability to guide the team through difficult situations.

Building trusting relationships is also reinforced by recognition and appreciation. A leader who recognizes and values the contributions of others, who shows gratitude for a job well done, and who celebrates successes is strengthening the relationship of trust. Recognition doesn't always have to be public or grandiose; Sometimes a simple word of thanks can have a significant impact. When people feel valued by their leader, their trust in them grows, as does their motivation to continue contributing to the team's success. Recognition also demonstrates that the leader is attentive to the efforts of others, which reinforces the perception that the leader is fair and equitable.

Finally, building trusting relationships takes time and patience. Trust is not established overnight; It is the result of a series of positive and coherent interactions over time. A leader must be willing to invest time in building and maintaining trust, through constant and meaningful actions. This includes being patient with others, understanding that trust can be fragile, and being willing to work to rebuild it if it is ever broken. Patience also means giving people the time they need to adapt, to learn, and to grow in their roles, knowing that trust will strengthen as the relationship develops.

In short, building trusting relationships is essential for any leader seeking to guide their team effectively. Trust is based on integrity, transparency, active listening, empathy, consistency, the ability to trust others, fair handling of conflict, recognition and patience. A leader who cultivates trust creates a work environment in which people feel safe, valued, and motivated to do their best. This type of environment not only improves team performance, but also fosters a sense of community and collaboration that is essential for long-term success. By understanding and applying the principles of building trusting relationships, leaders can strengthen their ability to influence, inspire, and guide their teams toward meaningful and lasting achievements.

Influence without Authority

Influence without authority is one of the most interesting yet powerful challenges a leader can face. In many situations, especially at the beginning of a career or in a new environment, you do not have the title or formal power that comes with a leadership position. However, this does not mean that you cannot have a significant impact on others or the direction a project or organization takes. In fact, the ability to influence without authority is one of the most valuable skills a leader can develop, as it is based on the ability to persuade, motivate and guide others without depending on the power that a formal position grants.

Influence without authority begins with personal credibility. People tend to follow those they respect and trust. This credibility is not earned with a title, but with consistent actions, knowledge, and the demonstration of a genuine commitment to shared goals. When someone demonstrates competence in their work, offers valuable solutions, and delivers on their promises, they begin to build a reputation for trustworthiness. This reputation is the basis of influence, as others will be more willing to listen to, consider, and follow the recommendations of someone who has proven themselves to be competent and trustworthy.

In addition to credibility, influence without authority also depends on the ability to build strong relationships. Relationships are the bridge that allows a person to influence others, even without having formal power. This involves taking the time to get to know people, understanding their motivations, concerns and aspirations, and showing a genuine interest in their well-being. People are more likely to be influenced by someone who demonstrates empathy and understanding than by someone who simply tries to impose their will. By building relationships based on mutual respect and collaboration, you create an environment where influence flows naturally as people feel they are working together toward a common goal.

Another key tool to influence without authority is effective communication. The way an idea is presented can be as important as the idea itself. A leader who knows how to communicate her vision clearly, persuasively, and tailored to the audience has a significant advantage when it comes to influencing others. This involves not only speaking eloquently, but also actively listening and adapting the message so that it resonates with the concerns and aspirations of those who hear it. Effective communication also includes the ability to articulate the benefits of an idea or action, not only to the organization, but also to the individuals involved. When people see how something benefits them personally, they are more willing to support and follow that idea.

The ability to influence without authority also relies on the ability to lead by example. Actions speak louder than words, and when someone demonstrates the behavior they expect from others, those behaviors are more likely to be adopted. This means being proactive, taking responsibility, and working with dedication and enthusiasm. When others see that someone is willing to go the extra mile, face challenges, and maintain a positive attitude, they are more likely to follow that example. Leading by example does not require formal authority, but it does require integrity and consistency in every action.

Persuasion is another important aspect of influence without authority. Persuasion is the art of convincing others to support an idea or take a specific action. Unlike coercion, which is based on pressure or power, persuasion is based on logic, emotion, and credibility. To persuade someone, it is crucial to understand their perspective and what motivates them. This allows you to present arguments that will resonate with your values and interests. Additionally, effective persuasion often involves telling stories or giving examples that make the idea more tangible and relatable. When you can connect with people's emotions and experiences, you are more likely to gain their support.

Teamwork is another fundamental aspect to influence without authority. In many cases, influence is best exerted when working collaboratively with others. This involves not only making suggestions or proposing ideas, but also actively engaging in the implementation process. When someone is seen as a valuable collaborator and not just an observer or critic, their ideas are more likely to be accepted and their influence to grow. Teamwork also allows for sharing credit for successes, which strengthens relationships and increases others' willingness to follow informal leadership in the future.

Adaptability is another key skill in influence without authority. Situations change, and an effective leader must be able to adjust his or her approach depending on the circumstances. This might mean changing strategy if an idea is not being well received, or being flexible about working methods to accommodate the needs of others. Adaptability also means being open to new ideas and perspectives, and being willing to learn from others. When someone shows that they are adaptable and able to adjust their approach to achieve the best results, they gain the respect of others, which in turn increases their ability to influence.

Another valuable tool is the use of constructive feedback. The ability to give and receive feedback effectively is crucial to influencing without authority. When feedback is given in a respectful and helpful manner, it demonstrates a commitment to the development and success of others. This not only strengthens relationships, but also sets a tone of mutual respect and collaboration. Additionally, being willing to receive feedback and act on it shows humility and openness, qualities that increase credibility and the ability to influence others.

It is also important to mention patience as an essential component of influence without authority. Changing minds and hearts doesn't always happen overnight. It may take time for ideas to be accepted and for people to feel comfortable following informal leadership. A leader who knows how to influence without authority must be patient and persistent, maintaining focus on his or her goals and continuing the effort even when the results are not immediate. Patience also means being willing to repeat important messages, reinforce ideas, and be available to support others in their own decision-making process.

Influence without authority also requires a service mentality. A leader who seeks to influence from a place of service to others, and not self-aggrandizement, is more effective in generating positive change. This means putting the needs of the team and the organization above one's own ambitions, and working to support others in their success. When people see that someone is genuinely committed to their well-being and success, they are more willing to follow their leadership, even if they have no formal authority. The service mindset creates a dynamic of trust and reciprocity that is critical to influence.

Finally, influence without authority involves being willing to share credit for achievements. A leader who influences without authority understands that success is the result of a collective effort and does not seek to monopolize recognition. Sharing credit not only strengthens relationships, but also motivates others to continue working together toward common goals. This collaborative approach reinforces the idea that leadership is not about a title or power, but rather the ability to work with others to achieve positive impact. The willingness to share success and recognize everyone's contributions is a sign of a mature and confident leader who understands the true meaning of influence.

In short, influence without authority is a crucial skill for any leader, since one does not always have the formal power to guide others. This influence is built through credibility, strong relationships, effective communication, leadership by example, persuasion, teamwork, adaptability, constructive feedback, patience, service mentality, and willingness to share the credit. By developing and applying these skills, anyone can effectively influence, motivate others, and lead their team to success, regardless of their formal position in the organization.

An Underrated Leadership Skill

In the world of leadership, many skills stand out as essential: the ability to make decisions, strategic vision, effective communication, among others. However, there is one skill that is often underestimated, but is essential for any leader who wants to have a lasting impact: the ability to listen. Listening, although it may seem simple or secondary, is actually one of the most powerful tools a leader can possess. It's not just about hearing what others say, but about truly understanding, processing and acting on that information. This skill, when consciously cultivated and practiced, can transform the way a leader connects with her team, makes decisions, and guides her organization.

Listening is much more than simply paying attention to another person's words. It is an active process that requires focus, empathy, and a deliberate effort to understand the context, emotions, and intentions behind what is being said. A leader who listens well is able to pick up on the subtleties of a conversation, notice what is not explicitly said, and read between the lines to gain a more complete understanding of the situation. This type of deep listening not only improves communication, but also strengthens relationships as people feel truly heard and understood. When a leader demonstrates that he values what others have to say, an environment of trust and mutual respect is generated, which in turn fosters collaboration and commitment.

One of the reasons listening skills are underrated is because they are often associated with passivity. In a world that values action, speaking, deciding and doing, listening can seem like a secondary or even unnecessary activity. However, nothing could be further from the truth. Listening is an active form of leadership, as it allows the leader to gather the information necessary to make informed decisions, understand the needs and concerns of his or her team, and detect potential problems before they become crises. Active listening is actually a form of proactive leadership, as it allows the leader to anticipate challenges and respond effectively to opportunities.

Another reason listening is underrated is because it is often confused with simply being present in a conversation. But active listening is much more than that. It involves not only paying attention to the words, but also to the gestures, tone of voice, body language and emotions that accompany what is said. It is a skill that requires concentration and conscious effort to not only capture the literal message, but also the emotional and contextual subtext. A leader who masters the skill of listening is able to understand the true concerns of his team, even when they are not expressed directly. This allows you to respond more effectively and make decisions that consider both the facts and the emotions involved.

Listening is also essential for conflict resolution, a task that all leaders face at some point. Conflicts often arise when people feel that they are not being heard or understood. A leader who can actively listen to all parties involved has a better chance of mediating and finding a solution that satisfies everyone. By demonstrating that each person's perspectives are valued, the leader not only resolves conflict more effectively, but also strengthens team cohesion. The skill of listening in conflict situations not only defuses tensions, but also creates an environment in which people feel safer to express their concerns in the future, knowing that they will be listened to respectfully.

Additionally, the ability to listen is intrinsically linked to empathy, another key leadership skill. Listening with empathy means putting yourself in the other person's shoes, trying to understand their perspective and feeling what they feel. This type of listening not only strengthens the relationship between the leader and his or her team, but also allows the leader to make more humane and equitable decisions. A leader who listens with empathy is able to recognize the emotions and needs of her team, allowing her to respond in a way that fosters trust and mutual respect. Empathy, fueled by active listening, creates an environment in which people feel valued not only for what they do, but also for who they are.

Another important aspect of listening is that it allows the leader to learn and grow. No leader has all the answers, and those who recognize this and are willing to listen to others have a significant advantage. Listening to others allows the leader to access new ideas, perspectives and knowledge that can enrich his or her own understanding and improve her ability to make decisions. A leader who listens to his or her team, colleagues, and other stakeholders is constantly learning and adapting, allowing him or her to stay relevant and effective in an ever-changing environment. This type of continuous learning is essential for any leader who wants to have a lasting impact.

The ability to listen is also crucial to motivating and engaging a team. People want to feel valued and heard, and when a leader demonstrates that he is willing to listen to their ideas, concerns, and suggestions, they feel more motivated to contribute to the team's success. Listening is a way to recognize the importance of each team member, which in turn fosters a sense of belonging and commitment. A team that feels heard is a team that is willing to work harder, innovate, and overcome challenges, because they know that their leader values her input and is willing to support her efforts.

Additionally, active listening is essential for inclusive decision making. A leader who listens to his or her team before making important decisions not only gains more information, but also ensures that decisions are more inclusive and represent the perspectives of everyone involved. This not only improves the quality of decisions, but also increases acceptance and commitment to them. People are more likely to support a decision when they feel that they have been part of the decision-making process and that their opinion has been considered. Listening to others not only improves decisions, but also strengthens the sense of community and collaboration within the team.

Finally, the ability to listen is essential for innovation. The best ideas often emerge from conversations, discussions, and the exchange of ideas between people with different perspectives and experiences. A leader who actively listens is able to capture these ideas and foster an environment in which innovation can flourish. Listening allows the leader to identify opportunities, detect problems before they become obstacles, and create an environment in which people feel safe to propose new and challenging ideas. Innovation is not just about having great ideas, but also about listening to and nurturing the ideas of others, and this is only possible when active listening is a central part of the leadership style.

In conclusion, the ability to listen is an underrated, but absolutely essential, leadership skill. Active listening allows the leader to better understand their team, make more informed decisions, resolve conflicts effectively, learn and grow, motivate and engage their team, make inclusive decisions, and foster innovation. Although often overlooked in favor of flashier skills like decision-making or strategic vision, the ability to listen is what truly distinguishes an effective leader from a mediocre one. By cultivating and practicing the skill of listening, a leader can not only improve his or her own effectiveness, but also create an environment in which everyone feels valued, respected, and motivated to do their best.

Why Do You Want to Be a Leader?

Why do you want to be a leader? It's a simple question, but its answer can reveal a lot about your true motivation and purpose. Wanting to be a leader is a common aspiration, but the reasons behind this desire can vary widely. Some people seek leadership for the recognition or prestige that comes with it, while others are motivated by a genuine desire to help others reach their full potential. Whatever the reason, it is important to reflect deeply on it, as the motivation behind your desire to be a leader will influence how you exercise that leadership and the impact you will have on those around you.

A common reason why many want to be leaders is power. Power can be a very powerful tool when used correctly, but it can also be dangerous if pursued for the wrong reasons. Some people see leadership as a way to gain control over others, impose their will, and feel important. However, this type of motivation often leads to authoritarian and ineffective leadership. Power alone is not enough to be a good leader. In fact, the most effective leaders focus not on the power they have, but on how they can use it to serve others and for the common good. If your main motivation for being a leader is power, it is important to stop and reflect on how you plan to use that power and whether you are willing to take on the responsibility that comes with it.

Another reason someone might want to be a leader is the desire to make a difference. This is a nobler and often more effective motive. Leaders who are motivated by a genuine desire to improve their environment, help people grow, and make the world a better place tend to be more engaged and have a more positive impact. These leaders do not seek personal recognition, but rather focus on results and the well-being of others. The desire to make a difference is what drives many leaders to overcome challenges and keep going, even when things get tough. If your motivation for being a leader is this desire for positive impact, you are on the right path, but it is important to remember that this type of leadership also requires sacrifice, patience, and a constant focus on long-term goals.

The desire to be a leader can also be motivated by the search for personal growth. Leading others is a powerful way to learn about yourself, develop skills, and face challenges that push you outside your comfort zone. Leadership is an opportunity to grow both personally and professionally, and many aspire to lead because they see it as a way to become the best version of themselves. This is a valid and valuable motivation, but it is crucial not to lose sight that leadership is not just about you, but also about others. Growing as a leader means being willing to listen, learn from others, and put the team's needs above your own when necessary. If you are motivated by personal growth, be sure to balance this with a genuine commitment to the development and well-being of the people you lead.

Some people want to be leaders because they enjoy the challenge. Leading is not easy, and those who constantly seek new and stimulating challenges may see leadership as an opportunity to prove themselves. Leading involves making difficult decisions, navigating complex situations, and managing the pressure of being responsible for a team's success or failure. This type of challenge can be exciting for those who thrive in high-pressure environments and enjoy solving difficult problems. However, it is important to remember that leadership is not only a personal challenge, but also a responsibility towards others. If your motivation is to face challenges, make sure you are also prepared to assume the responsibility that comes with leading others, including the emotional and professional well-being of your team.

Another reason someone might want to be a leader is the desire to guide and teach others. For some, the greatest satisfaction from leadership comes from seeing others grow and develop under their guidance. This type of leader acts as a mentor, sharing their knowledge and experience to help others reach their potential. If you are motivated by this desire to guide and teach, you are ideally positioned to be an effective leader, as this type of leadership fosters an environment of continuous learning and personal development. However, it is important to remember that being a good mentor also means being willing to learn from others and accepting that each person has their own path and pace of growth.

Mentoring-based leadership is a journey of mutual learning, where both the leader and those led grow together.

Recognition and prestige are also common motivations for those who want to be leaders. There is no denying that leadership often carries a certain level of recognition, as leaders are visible and their achievements are often publicly recognized. However, leading by prestige alone can be a dangerous trap. Effective leadership is not about receiving applause or being in the spotlight, but about doing the work necessary to guide a team to success. If recognition is your main motivation, you may face disappointment, since leadership often involves hard work and not always visible. Additionally, leading only to be recognized can lead to selfish decisions and a disconnection from the real needs of the team. It is crucial that the desire for recognition be balanced with a genuine commitment to the work and the people you lead.

For some, leadership is an opportunity to leave a legacy. They want to be remembered for something meaningful, for having made a lasting contribution. This motivation can be very powerful, as it drives leaders to think long-term and make decisions that not only benefit their team or organization in the present, but also have a positive impact in the future. The desire to leave a legacy is a noble motivation, but it is important to remember that a legacy is not built overnight. It requires consistency, commitment, and a constant focus on the values and principles that guide your leadership. If your motivation is to leave a legacy, it is essential that you stay true to your values and always put the common good above personal interests.

You may also want to be a leader because you are passionate about a specific issue or cause. Leaders who are passionate about a cause often have a significant impact because they are deeply committed and motivated by something bigger than themselves. This passion can inspire others and create real movement or change. If you are motivated by a cause, it is important that you keep that passion alive and channel it in a constructive way. However, it is also crucial to remember that passion alone is not enough. You need to combine it with leadership skills, strategy and the ability to listen and adapt to the needs of your team. Passion must be the engine that drives your leadership, but you must also be willing to do the work necessary to turn that passion into concrete results.

Finally, you may want to be a leader because you feel it is your calling. Some people feel a natural calling toward leadership, as if they were destined to guide others. This sense of calling can be a powerful source of motivation, driving leaders to act with purpose and determination. However, even if you feel that leadership is your destiny, it is important to remember that leadership is a continuous journey of learning and growth. You must be willing to work on yourself, develop your skills and always be open to learning from the experiences and people around you. Leadership is not a final destination, but rather a continuous process of personal and professional evolution.

In conclusion, it is essential that you take the time to reflect on why you want to be a leader. The motivation behind your desire to lead will influence how you exercise that leadership and the impact you will have on others. Whether you are motivated by power, a desire to make a difference, personal growth, challenge, guidance from others, recognition, legacy, passion for a cause, or a sense of calling, the most important thing is that you motivation is aligned with a purpose greater than yourself. Leadership is a responsibility and a privilege, and those who lead with integrity, empathy, and a focus on the common good are the ones who truly leave a lasting mark.

Create an Inspiring Future

Creating an inspiring future is one of the most important and challenging tasks a leader faces. When we think of leadership, it is common to imagine someone who makes important decisions, manages teams, and solves problems. However, an essential aspect of leadership that is often overlooked is the ability to imagine and build a future that inspires others to move forward, even in times of uncertainty. A leader who is able to create an inspiring vision not only guides her team in the present, but also gives them a sense of purpose and direction that motivates them to work toward something bigger than themselves.

The first step to creating an inspiring future is having a clear vision. This vision doesn't have to be grand or complicated, but it does have to be powerful enough to resonate with people and motivate them to take action. An inspiring vision is one that connects with the values and aspirations of those who listen to it. It's not just about what you want to achieve as a leader, but what that vision represents for the team, organization, or community at large. An inspiring future is one in which everyone can see themselves, where each team member feels that they have an important role to play and that their work contributes to a greater goal.

Once you have defined a clear vision, the next step is to communicate it effectively. It's not enough to have a great idea in your mind; you must be able to articulate that idea in a way that others understand it and are inspired by it. Effective communication is key to creating an inspiring future. This involves not only sharing the vision, but also explaining why it is important, how it can be achieved, and what role each person will play in realizing it. It is important to be transparent and honest when communicating the vision, recognizing the challenges that will arise, but also highlighting the opportunities and benefits that will come from achieving it. The way you present your vision can make a big difference in how it is received and the motivation it generates in others.

A leader who wants to create an inspiring future must also be willing to listen and adapt their vision as necessary. An inspiring vision is not static; It must evolve as circumstances change and new ideas develop. Listening to your team and being open to their input is key to ensuring the vision remains relevant and meaningful to everyone. Additionally, when people feel that they have contributed to the creation of the vision, they are more committed to it and more willing to work to make it a reality. Inclusion and collaboration are key aspects in building an inspiring future.

Another important part of creating an inspiring future is demonstrating an unwavering commitment to the vision. As a leader, your attitude and behavior serve as a model for others. If you want people to believe in the future you are imagining, you must be the first to demonstrate your faith in that vision through your actions. This means being consistent in your decisions, maintaining a focus on the long term, and being willing to make sacrifices when necessary to stay on track toward your desired future. The leader's commitment is what gives credibility to the vision and what inspires others to keep going, even when things get difficult.

In addition to communicating and committing to the vision, it is essential that as a leader you also take concrete steps to begin building that future. An inspiring future is not created with words alone, but with actions. This means developing plans and strategies that bring you closer to the vision, setting clear and achievable goals, and making decisions that are aligned with the future you want to create. These actions not only demonstrate your commitment to the vision, but also show others that the future you imagine is possible. Seeing tangible progress, even if it is small, can be incredibly motivating for a team and reinforces the belief that they are on the right path.

It's important to remember that creating an inspiring future also means facing challenges and overcoming obstacles. No path to a better future is easy or free of difficulties. Part of a leader's job is to anticipate these challenges and prepare the team to meet them. This requires resilience, adaptability, and a growth mindset. Leaders who can keep the vision alive even in difficult times, who can motivate their team to persevere, and who find creative ways to overcome obstacles are those who truly succeed in creating an inspiring future. The ability to remain steadfast and optimistic in the face of adversity is what distinguishes great leaders.

Another key aspect of creating an inspiring future is making sure it is inclusive. A truly inspiring future is one where all voices are heard and valued. This means that, as a leader, you should strive to build a vision that is representative of the diverse perspectives and experiences within your team or organization. Inclusion not only enriches the vision, but also ensures that everyone feels part of the process and is motivated to contribute. Creating a future that is inclusive and equitable is essential for long-term success, as it fosters a sense of belonging and commitment in everyone involved.

Finally, a leader who wants to create an inspiring future must be able to celebrate successes and learn from failures. Every step towards realizing the vision should be recognized and celebrated, no matter how small. These moments of celebration not only reinforce commitment to the vision, but also serve as a reminder of how far they have come and what is possible. At the same time, failures and setbacks should be seen as learning opportunities. Instead of becoming discouraged, an inspiring leader uses failures as an opportunity to adjust vision, learn, and grow. This positive and resilient approach is what keeps inspiration alive and what motivates the team to move forward.

In short, creating an inspiring future is a process that requires a clear vision, effective communication, unwavering commitment, the ability to take action, a willingness to face challenges, the inclusion of diverse perspectives, and the ability to celebrate successes and learn from the failures. It is an ongoing journey that requires dedication and effort, but can have a deep and lasting impact on those you lead. An inspiring future is not only a goal to achieve, but a path that is built day by day with every decision, action and attitude you take as a leader. By creating an inspiring future, you not only guide your team toward a better destiny, but you also give them the courage and motivation to be an active part of that process, working together to realize a shared and meaningful vision.

Lead with Principles

Leading with principles is essential for anyone who aspires to be an authentic and respected leader. Principles are the fundamental norms or values that guide our actions, decisions and behavior. They are the foundation on which a leader's integrity and credibility are built. When you lead with principles, you not only set a high standard for yourself, but you also inspire others to follow those same values, creating an environment of trust, respect and collaboration.

One of the most important aspects of leading with principles is consistency. A leader who acts in accordance with his principles, regardless of the circumstances, demonstrates consistency and firmness in his decisions. This means that no matter if you are facing an easy or difficult situation, you will always make decisions based on the same core values. This consistency builds trust, as the people around you know they can count on you to act predictably and fairly. An inconsistent leader, who changes his principles as it suits him, quickly loses the trust of his team, since no one really knows what to expect from him.

Another crucial aspect of leading with principles is honesty. Honesty is one of the most valued principles in any area of life, and in leadership it is no exception. An honest leader earns the respect of others because he tells the truth, even when it is difficult or uncomfortable. Being honest not only means not lying, but also being transparent in your intentions and actions. A leader who is honest with his team creates an environment where people feel safe to express themselves, ask questions, and share their ideas. Honesty encourages openness and dialogue, which is essential for problem solving and innovation.

Integrity is another fundamental principle in leadership. Integrity refers to the ability to act in accordance with your values and principles, even when no one is looking. It's easy to follow your principles when everything is going well, but the true test of a leader is how he acts in times of pressure or temptation. A leader with integrity does not compromise or make concessions when it comes to his principles. Maintaining integrity means making difficult decisions, even if it means sacrificing something in the short term. A leader with integrity is a role model, not only for what he says, but for what he does.

Respect is an essential principle for any leader who aspires to create a positive and productive environment. Leading with respect means valuing each person as an individual, regardless of their position, background or abilities. A respectful leader actively listens to her team, considers her opinions, and treats everyone with dignity. Respect also means being aware of differences and being willing to learn from them. A leader who shows respect earns the respect of others, creating a positive cycle of trust and collaboration. Respect not only strengthens relationships within the team, but also fosters a sense of belonging and motivation.

Responsibility is another key principle in leadership. A responsible leader not only takes responsibility for his own actions, but also takes responsibility for the well-being and success of his team. This means being willing to accept the consequences of your decisions, both good and bad, and being prepared to make necessary adjustments when things don't go as expected. Responsibility also involves being proactive in solving problems and identifying opportunities for improvement. A responsible leader does not make excuses or blame others when something goes wrong, but instead focuses on finding solutions and learning from experiences.

Justice is an essential principle for any leader who aspires to be fair and objective in their decisions. Leading with justice means treating everyone equally, without favoritism or prejudice. A fair leader evaluates people and situations based on facts and merits, not personal preferences or assumptions. Fairness also means being transparent in decision-making processes and communication with the team. A leader who acts fairly fosters an environment of equity, where everyone has the same opportunities for success and where effort and dedication are valued. Fairness is the basis of trust and mutual respect in any team.

Commitment is another principle that guides effective leaders. A committed leader is dedicated to their vision, their team, and the goals they have set out to achieve. This commitment is reflected in the leader's willingness to work hard, overcome obstacles, and persevere even when things get difficult. Commitment also means being available to your team, offering support and guidance when needed, and always being willing to step up in times of need. A committed leader inspires his team to stay focused and move forward, even in the most challenging circumstances.

The principle of empathy is fundamental in leadership. Leading with empathy means putting yourself in the shoes of others, understanding their perspectives and concerns, and responding in a compassionate and understanding way. Empathy not only improves relationships within the team, but also allows the leader to make more informed and sensitive decisions. An empathetic leader creates an environment where people feel valued and understood, which in turn fosters loyalty and commitment. Empathy also helps a leader manage conflict more effectively, as it allows a better understanding of the emotions and motivations of the people involved.

The principle of humility is crucial for any leader who wants to stay connected with their team and continually learn. A humble leader recognizes that he does not have all the answers and is willing to listen and learn from others, regardless of their position or experience. Humility also means being willing to admit mistakes and accept constructive criticism. A humble leader does not seek personal recognition, but rather the success of the team as a whole. This humble, team-oriented approach creates an environment of collaboration and trust, where everyone feels empowered to contribute and grow.

Finally, the principle of service is central to leadership. Leading with a spirit of service means putting the needs of others above your own and being willing to make sacrifices to support the team's success. A leader who serves his team not only leads from the top, but also works alongside them, supporting and guiding them every step of the way. This service approach creates a sense of unity and common purpose, where each team member feels that he is working toward a shared goal. A leader who serves his team inspires loyalty, respect, and a strong sense of community.

In conclusion, leading with principles is essential for anyone who wants to be an authentic, respected and effective leader. Principles such as consistency, honesty, integrity, respect, responsibility, fairness, commitment, empathy, humility and service form the foundation on which solid and lasting leadership is built. These principles not only guide your actions and decisions as a leader, but they also set the tone for the entire team, creating an environment where trust, collaboration, and mutual respect thrive. Leading with principles is not always easy, but it is what sets great leaders apart from others and ensures a positive, lasting impact on the people and organizations they serve.

Overcoming Leadership Challenges

Overcoming leadership challenges is a task that requires not only skills and knowledge, but also a great deal of resilience, creativity and determination. The leadership path is filled with obstacles, both large and small, and a leader's ability to face and overcome them is what defines their long-term success. Although each challenge is unique and may require different approaches, there are some fundamental principles and strategies that can help you navigate these difficult times and come out stronger on the other side.

The first step in overcoming leadership challenges is to recognize that these challenges are inevitable. No matter how prepared you are or how much experience you have, there will always be times when you are faced with difficult situations that will test your skills as a leader. It is important to understand that these challenges are not signs of failure, but rather opportunities to learn, grow and improve. Adopting this mindset allows you to approach problems with a more positive and proactive attitude, rather than feeling overwhelmed or defeated.

One of the most common challenges in leadership is making difficult decisions. Often, as a leader, you will find yourself in the position of having to make decisions that will be unpopular or that will involve sacrifices for you or your team. These decisions can range from budget cuts to strategic changes that alter the direction of the organization. To overcome these types of challenges, it is essential that you stay true to your principles and values. Making decisions based on what is fair and right, rather than what is easy or convenient, is what defines a true leader. Additionally, it is important to communicate your decisions clearly and transparently, explaining the reasons behind them and how they will benefit the team or organization in the long term.

Another significant challenge in leadership is conflict management. Conflicts are inevitable in any team or organization, whether due to differences of opinion, clashing personalities, or unmet expectations. As a leader, it is your responsibility to mediate these conflicts fairly and effectively, ensuring that they are not only resolved, but also used as opportunities to improve team dynamics. The key to overcoming this challenge is to develop communication and empathy skills. Actively listening to all parties involved, understanding their concerns, and finding common ground are essential steps in resolving conflicts. Additionally, it is important to address problems in a timely manner, before they escalate and cause more damage.

Pressure and stress are constant challenges in leadership. Making important decisions, managing teams, and meeting the expectations of superiors can be significant sources of stress. However, learning to manage stress is crucial to maintaining long-term effectiveness and well-being. One of the best ways to overcome this challenge is to develop stress management techniques, such as meditation, regular exercise, and effective planning. Additionally, it is essential that you learn to delegate tasks and trust your team. Trying to do everything yourself is not only unsustainable, but it can also lead to rapid burnout. Delegating not only eases your burden, it also empowers your team members, allowing them to grow and develop their own leadership skills.

Change is another important challenge that every leader will face at some point. Changes can be internal, such as a team restructuring, or external, such as an economic crisis or changes in the industry. Regardless of the type of change, the ability to adapt and guide your team through it is a crucial leadership skill. Overcoming the challenge of change requires flexibility and an open mind. You must be willing to adjust your plans and strategies as necessary, and maintain a positive attitude in the face of uncertainty. Additionally, it's important to clearly communicate the reason for the change to your team, making sure they understand its purpose and how they will be affected. Involving your team in the change process, asking for their opinions and concerns, can also help smooth the transition and encourage greater acceptance.

Loneliness is a less obvious, but no less important challenge in leadership. Leaders often find themselves in positions where they must make difficult decisions without being able to share their doubts or concerns with others. This feeling of loneliness can be draining and affect both decision-making and the emotional well-being of the leader. To overcome this challenge, it is essential to build a support network, whether inside or outside the organization. Having someone you can talk openly with about your challenges and concerns can make a big difference. Additionally, participating in leadership groups or seeking mentorship can provide you with new perspectives and emotional support. You shouldn't be afraid to ask for help or advice when you need it; Even the most successful leaders depend on others for support and guidance.

Resistance to change from others is another common leadership challenge. When you introduce new ideas or strategies, you are likely to encounter resistance, whether due to fear of the unknown or attachment to traditional ways of doing things. Overcoming this challenge requires patience, persuasion and persistence. It is important to present your ideas clearly and convincingly, highlighting the benefits they will bring. Additionally, involving people in the change process, allowing them to express their concerns and contribute their ideas, can help reduce resistance and increase acceptance. Sometimes change can take time, and it's crucial not to be discouraged by initial resistance. Maintaining a positive approach and being willing to adjust your approach as necessary can help you overcome this challenge.

Making decisions under uncertainty is another challenge that leaders often face. In a world where information can be incomplete or contradictory, making decisions can be extremely difficult. However, uncertainty should not paralyze you. To overcome this challenge, it is essential to develop a tolerance for risk and ambiguity. This means being willing to make decisions based on the best information available, even when you don't have all the answers. It is also helpful to develop contingency plans and be prepared to adjust your course if circumstances change. The ability to make quick and effective decisions under uncertainty is what separates great leaders from others.

Finally, one of the most important challenges of leadership is maintaining team motivation and morale. As challenges pile up, it's easy for the team to feel unmotivated or discouraged. As a leader, it is your responsibility to maintain energy and focus on goals. Overcoming this challenge involves modeling optimism and resilience, celebrating successes, no matter how small, and providing support and recognition when needed. It's also important to maintain open and honest communication with your team, ensuring they understand the importance of their work and how it contributes to overall success. Motivation is contagious, and a motivated leader can inspire their team to keep going, even in the most difficult times.

In short, overcoming leadership challenges is a complex task that requires a combination of skills, strategies and attitudes. From making difficult decisions to managing conflict, managing stress, adapting to change and maintaining team motivation, every challenge presents an opportunity to grow and develop as a leader. By facing these challenges with a positive mindset, a proactive approach, and a commitment to your principles, you will not only be able to overcome them, but you will also become stronger and prepare to face future challenges with greater confidence and effectiveness. Leading is not always easy, but it is through these challenges that truly great leaders are forged and leave a lasting legacy.

Development of Decision Making Skills

Developing decision-making skills is one of the most important competencies any leader must cultivate. The ability to make effective and timely decisions is crucial to the success of a team, an organization, and even in one's personal life. However, decision making is not something that can be done randomly; It requires a well-thought-out process, careful analysis, and often a good dose of intuition and experience. In this chapter, we'll explore how you can develop and hone your decision-making skills, ensuring that every decision you make is informed, deliberate, and effective.

The first step to improving your decision-making skills is to understand that not all decisions are created equal. Some decisions are simple and have a minor impact, while others are complex and can have significant long-term consequences. Knowing how to distinguish between different types of decisions and their importance is essential. Routine decisions, such as choosing which tasks to prioritize on a given day, require less time and analysis than strategic decisions, such as changing the direction of a project or hiring a new team member. Being able to identify the type of decision you are facing will help you determine how much attention and resources you need to devote to it.

Once you have identified the type of decision, the next step is to gather the necessary information. Making decisions based on assumptions or incomplete information can lead to costly mistakes. Therefore, it is essential that you gather all the relevant data and knowledge before making a decision. This includes consulting experts, reviewing relevant documents or reports, and speaking with people who will be affected by the decision. The more information you have at your disposal, the better you can evaluate the options and possible outcomes. However, it's also important to avoid analysis paralysis, which occurs when you spend so much time gathering information that you never make a decision. Learning to balance the need for information with the need for action is key to effective decision making.

Analysis of options is another crucial component in the decision-making process.

You will rarely have just one option to consider; In most cases, you will have several alternatives, each with its own advantages and disadvantages. To analyze these options, it is helpful to make a list of pros and cons for each. This exercise will allow you to clearly visualize the benefits and risks associated with each option. Additionally, it is helpful to consider the short- and long-term implications of each decision. An option that seems attractive in the short term could have negative consequences in the long term, and vice versa. Taking the time to think about how each option will affect the future is essential to making well-informed decisions.

Another useful strategy in decision making is the use of what-if scenarios. Imagining different scenarios and how they would play out depending on the decision you make can give you a clearer view of possible outcomes. For example, if you are considering implementing a new process on your team, you could imagine a scenario where everything goes as planned and another where unforeseen problems arise. By considering these scenarios, you can prepare contingency plans or adjust your decision to minimize risks. Using scenarios allows you to be better prepared to handle any outcomes that may arise.

The next step in the decision-making process is risk assessment. Every decision carries a level of risk, and it is important that you are aware of these risks before making a final decision. Assessing risk involves considering how likely a negative outcome is to occur and what impact it would have if it did occur. Some decisions may involve low risks with minor consequences, while others may have high risks with significant consequences. When assessing risks, it is crucial that you consider both tangible and intangible aspects. Financial risks, for example, are easy to quantify, but risks related to team morale or organizational reputation may be more difficult to assess, although no less important.

After you have gathered the information, analyzed the options and evaluated the risks, it is time to make the decision. This is perhaps the most difficult step, as it involves committing to an option and moving forward with it. It's natural to feel uncertain at this point, especially if the decision has big implications. However, it is important to remember that no decision is risk-free, and uncertainty is part of the process. What sets a good leader apart is the ability to make decisions with confidence, even when you don't have all the answers. It is at this moment when intuition and experience play a crucial role. Often, your gut will tell you which option is best, based on your prior knowledge and understanding of the context.

Once you have made the decision, the next step is to implement it. The execution of the decision is as important as the decision itself. A well-made decision can fail if it is not implemented correctly. It is essential that you clearly communicate your decision to all parties involved, explaining the reasoning behind it and the steps that will follow. Additionally, you should ensure that everyone understands their roles and responsibilities in implementing the decision. Planning and coordination are key at this stage to ensure that the decision is executed effectively and efficiently. It is also important to be prepared to adjust the plan if problems arise during implementation.

The last step in the decision-making process is evaluation and learning. After the decision has been implemented, it is essential that you review the results to see if the decision had the desired effect. This involves comparing actual results with expected results and analyzing what worked well and what could have been done differently. This evaluation provides you with valuable learning that you can apply to future decisions. Even if the decision wasn't as successful as you hoped, it's important to view the process as an opportunity to learn and improve. Decision making is a skill that is honed over time, and every experience, good or bad, makes you a better decision maker.

In addition to following these steps, it is important that you work on developing a mindset of continuous improvement in your decision making. This means always being willing to learn new techniques and approaches, as well as seeking feedback from others. Participating in decision-making courses, reading about other leaders' experiences, and reflecting on your own past decisions are effective ways to improve your skills. Remember that decision making is not just a task you do from time to time; It is a fundamental skill that affects all aspects of your professional and personal life. By committing to continuous improvement, you will ensure that your decisions are increasingly accurate and effective.

In conclusion, developing decision-making skills is an ongoing process that requires practice, reflection, and constant learning. By understanding the different types of decisions, gathering the necessary information, analyzing options, evaluating risks, making decisions with confidence, implementing them effectively, and learning from the results, you can significantly improve your ability to make effective decisions. This skill will not only help you be a better leader, but will also allow you to navigate the challenges and opportunities that arise in life with greater confidence and success. Decision making is both an art and a science, and over time, you can master both aspects to become a confident and competent decision maker.

Evolve as a Leader

Evolving as a leader is a continuous and dynamic process that does not end once you reach a leadership position. On the contrary, it is the starting point for a journey of personal and professional growth that never stops. Evolution as a leader involves being constantly learning, adapting to new circumstances, improving your skills, and being increasingly aware of your impact on others. In this chapter, we will explore how you can evolve as a leader and why this constant development is essential to maintaining your relevance and effectiveness in any context.

The first aspect of evolving as a leader is constant self-evaluation. Being an effective leader requires that you know yourself, understand your strengths and weaknesses, and be willing to work on areas that need improvement. Self-assessment is not just superficial reflection; It is a deep and honest analysis of your performance, your decisions, and how you relate to others. Taking time to reflect on your experiences, receive feedback from your team and colleagues, and consider how you could have handled situations differently is crucial to your growth. Through self-assessment, you can identify patterns in your behavior and take steps to correct any negative trends before they become a bigger problem.

Continuing education is another fundamental pillar in the evolution of leadership. The world changes rapidly, and what worked yesterday may not be effective today. Leaders who get stuck in the past or who resist learning new things risk becoming obsolete. Therefore, it is essential that you are always looking for new opportunities to learn and expand your knowledge. This may include reading books and articles about leadership, attending conferences and workshops, or enrolling in professional development courses. Also, don't underestimate the value of informal learning, such as conversations with other leaders or observing how they handle their challenges. Every experience is an opportunity to learn something new, and the more you are willing to absorb, the faster you will evolve as a leader.

Adaptability is another crucial skill for leadership evolution. We live in a constantly changing world, where situations can transform quickly and without warning. A leader who is unable to adapt to new circumstances may quickly find himself overwhelmed by events. Adaptability not only means being flexible in your approach, but also being willing to abandon old ways of doing things if they are no longer effective. This may involve changing strategy, adopting new technologies, or even changing your leadership style to adapt to the needs of your team. The ability to adapt not only helps you meet challenges more effectively, but it also shows your team that you are committed to long-term success and not just maintaining the status quo.

Empathy is another fundamental aspect in the evolution of leadership. As you grow as a leader, you will realize that leading is not just about making decisions and directing others, but also about understanding the emotions, needs, and perspectives of the people around you. Empathy allows you to connect more deeply with your team, which in turn fosters trust and collaboration. Being an empathetic leader does not mean being soft or permissive, but rather being aware of how your actions and decisions affect others and being willing to adjust your approach for the well-being of the group. As you develop as a leader, working on your capacity for empathy will allow you to build stronger and more effective relationships with your team, which in turn will contribute to collective success.

Another important part of evolving as a leader is the ability to handle uncertainty. Leadership does not always offer clear answers, and you will often have to make decisions in situations where information is incomplete or contradictory. Uncertainty can be disconcerting, but it is an inevitable part of leadership. Learning to be comfortable with uncertainty and make informed decisions despite it is a sign of a mature and confident leader. This does not mean acting impulsively, but rather being able to assess the situation, weigh the risks and make the best possible decision with the information available. Over time, as you face more uncertain situations, you will develop greater confidence in your ability to navigate the unknown, allowing you to lead more effectively.

Developing a clear vision is also a key aspect in the evolution of leadership. An evolving leader not only responds to present circumstances, but also has a clear idea of where he wants to go and how he plans to get there. This vision not only guides you as a leader, but also inspires your team to work toward common goals. Developing a clear vision requires you to think long-term, consider the big picture, and be able to communicate your ideas in ways that others can understand and support. As you evolve, your vision may change and adapt, but the important thing is that you always have a sense of purpose and direction to guide you and your team.

Leadership also involves developing the ability to delegate. At first, many leaders tend to want to do everything themselves, either due to a lack of trust in others or fear that things will not be done the way they want. However, as you evolve as a leader, you will realize that delegating is not only necessary, but also beneficial. Delegating tasks allows other team members to develop their skills and take on more responsibilities, which in turn relieves your burden and allows you to focus on the most important strategic decisions. Delegating is also a show of trust in your team, which can increase morale and commitment. Learning to delegate effectively is a crucial step in your evolution as a leader.

Resilience is another vital component of leadership evolution. Being a leader is not easy; You will face challenges, failures and criticism along the way. Resilience is the ability to bounce back from these setbacks, learn from them, and move forward with determination. A resilient leader does not crumble in the face of adversity, but rather uses it as an opportunity to grow and improve. Developing resilience requires you to cultivate a positive mindset, seek support when you need it, and maintain a long-term perspective. Over time, you will realize that challenges are not insurmountable barriers, but rather stepping stones on your path to success.

Finally, evolving as a leader also means leaving a legacy. As you grow and develop in your leadership role, you should think about the lasting impact you want to have on your team, your organization, and beyond. What values and principles do you want to last? How do you want to be remembered as a leader? Leaving a legacy is not about achieving fame or personal glory, but about contributing significantly to the success and well-being of others. A truly evolved leader understands that his or her work is not measured only by tangible achievements, but by the positive and lasting impact it has on people and the organization. This legacy is what truly defines your success as a leader and what will inspire future generations to follow your example.

In short, evolving as a leader is an ongoing process that involves self-assessment, continuing education, adaptability, empathy, managing uncertainty, developing a vision, effective delegation, resilience, and building a lasting legacy. It's not an easy path, but it is an incredibly rewarding journey that not only makes you a better leader, but also a better person. By committing to constantly evolve, you not only prepare yourself to face any challenge that comes your way, but you also inspire others to grow and develop alongside you. Ultimately, evolution as a leader is a never-ending journey, one that will take you to greater and greater heights if you remain open to learning and change.

Learn from Other Leaders

Learning from other leaders is one of the most powerful and effective ways to improve your own leadership skills. Leadership is an art that is honed through practice and observation, and by observing other leaders, you can gain valuable insights that you might not have otherwise discovered for yourself. This learning is not just limited to famous or historical leaders; It can come from anyone in a leadership position, whether it's a direct boss, a colleague, a mentor, or even an opinion leader in your community. By learning from others, you can avoid making the same mistakes they have made, adopt effective practices that have been proven to work, and broaden your perspective on what it means to be a good leader.

One of the most important aspects of learning from other leaders is observation. Close observation allows you to see how leaders handle various situations, how they interact with their teams, and how they make crucial decisions. When you watch a leader in action, pay attention to how they communicate their ideas, how they resolve conflicts, and how they inspire their teams. Pay attention to the details, such as body language, tone of voice, and word choice, because it is often these small details that make the difference in a leader's effectiveness. By observing different leaders in different situations, you can begin to identify patterns and techniques that you would like to incorporate into your own leadership style.

In addition to observing, another effective way to learn from other leaders is through mentoring. A mentor is someone who has already walked the leadership path and is willing to share their knowledge and experience with you. Having a mentor gives you the opportunity to receive direct, personalized feedback, which can accelerate your development as a leader. Find a mentor who not only has experience, but also shares your values and is willing to invest time in helping you grow. The mentoring relationship is a two-way learning path, where both can benefit from the exchange of ideas and experiences. As you grow as a leader, you can also become a mentor to others, perpetuating the cycle of learning and growth.

Reading is another invaluable tool for learning from other leaders. There are a vast number of books, articles, and biographies written by and about leaders who have left a significant mark in their fields. Reading about the experiences of these leaders allows you to access their knowledge and perspective without needing to interact with them directly. You can learn how they faced challenges, what strategies they used to achieve their goals, and what lessons they learned along the way. Additionally, reading about a variety of leaders exposes you to different leadership styles and approaches, helping you develop a broader understanding of what it means to be a leader. Don't just read about leaders in your field; Learning from leaders in different industries and contexts can offer you new ideas and approaches that can be applied in your own situation.

Another way to learn from other leaders is to participate in leadership networks. These may include focus groups, workshops, conferences and seminars where leaders come together to share their experiences and knowledge. Attending these events allows you to not only hear from established leaders, but also interact with them and ask specific questions about the challenges you face. Networking with other leaders also gives you the opportunity to learn from your peers, who may be facing similar challenges as you. These interactions can offer you new perspectives and solutions that you may not have considered. Additionally, being surrounded by other motivated and successful leaders can inspire you to raise your own leadership level.

Learning from other leaders can also be facilitated by observing leaders in action through the media. Today, with access to the internet and social media, it is easier than ever to see and hear leaders from around the world. You can follow leaders on platforms like LinkedIn, Twitter or YouTube, where they often share their thoughts, strategies and experiences in real time. Podcasts and webinars are also valuable resources where leaders discuss current issues and how they approach them from a leadership perspective. Consuming this content regularly allows you to stay up to date with trends in leadership and learn from a variety of voices and styles.

A crucial aspect of learning from other leaders is the ability to be critical and selective about what you learn. Not everything a leader does is applicable or appropriate for your situation. It is important that you analyze what you observe and determine what aligns with your own values and goals. It is not about blindly imitating other leaders, but about adapting the lessons learned to your own style and context. Sometimes learning from a leader means seeing what not to do. Even the most successful leaders make mistakes, and these mistakes can offer you valuable lessons about what to avoid or how to better handle a similar situation in the future. By being selective in what you adopt, you can build a leadership style that is authentic and effective.

In addition to learning from other leaders' successes, it is equally important to learn from their failures. All leaders, no matter how successful, have faced challenges and made mistakes. These failures, while difficult, are often where the deepest and most meaningful lessons are found. Reading or hearing about how a leader faced and overcame failure can provide you with guidance on how to handle your own challenges. It teaches you that failure is not the end, but a part of the growth process. Learning from the failures of others allows you to be better prepared to face your own obstacles with resilience and determination.

Finally, learning from other leaders also means applying what you have learned in your own context. Knowledge gained through observation, reading, mentoring, and leadership networks is not useful unless you put it into practice. This means experimenting with new ideas, strategies and approaches in your own leadership environment. Don't be afraid to try something new based on what you've learned from other leaders, even if you're not sure how it will turn out. The practical application is where the learning really solidifies and where you can adjust and refine your leadership skills. By applying what you have learned, you will also be contributing to your own continued growth and evolution as a leader.

In conclusion, learning from other leaders is a fundamental strategy for leadership development. Through observation, mentoring, reading, participating in leadership networks, and selective criticism, you can gain knowledge and skills that will help you be a more effective and well-rounded leader. Learning from others does not mean simply copying what they do, but adapting their lessons to your own style and context. By doing this, you not only improve as a leader, but you also prepare yourself to face future challenges with greater perspective and wisdom. Leadership is a journey of continuous learning, and by drawing on the experiences and insights of other leaders, you can move forward with greater confidence and success on that journey.

The Path to Formal Leadership

The path to formal leadership is a journey full of challenges, learning, and opportunities to grow. It is not a path that is taken overnight, nor is it just about obtaining a title or a position of authority. Being a formal leader involves constant preparation, both personally and professionally, to be able to guide others effectively and with purpose. In this chapter, we will explore the key stages on this path, from developing essential skills to building a strong vision that allows you to lead with confidence and success.

The first step on the path to formal leadership is self-knowledge. Before you can lead others, you must know yourself deeply. This involves understanding your strengths, your weaknesses, your values and your motivations. Self-awareness allows you to be aware of how your actions and decisions affect others and helps you maintain a clear perspective when facing challenges. This process of self-knowledge is not something that is done just once, but is continuous. As you face new experiences and situations, you will always have the opportunity to learn something new about yourself. By being in tune with your own identity, you can lead with authenticity and build more genuine and effective relationships with those you guide.

The next step on this path is the development of fundamental leadership skills. These skills include effective communication, decision making, empathy, conflict resolution, and the ability to inspire and motivate others. It is not just about acquiring theoretical knowledge, but about practicing these skills in daily life. Communication, for example, is not just about speaking clearly, but about actively listening, understanding different perspectives, and being able to convey ideas in ways that resonate with others. Decision making, for its part, requires a balance between rational analysis and intuition, considering both the data and the human impact of decisions. Empathy allows you to connect with people on a deeper level, understanding their emotions and needs, which is essential to building a cohesive and committed team. Conflict resolution is crucial to maintaining harmony and productivity in a team, and the ability to inspire and motivate is what really drives people to be their best.

As you develop these skills, it's important to also build your network. Leadership does not develop in a vacuum; It thrives on the relationships you build along the way. These relationships can include mentors, colleagues, friends, and other leaders who inspire you. A strong network not only provides you with support and advice, but also exposes you to different points of view and opens doors to new opportunities. Participating in focus groups, attending conferences and leadership events, and actively seeking connections with people from different industries and backgrounds can enrich your experience and provide you with a broader perspective. Additionally, these relationships allow you to observe how other leaders handle similar challenges and what strategies they use to succeed, which can be extremely valuable in your own development.

Building a clear vision is another crucial aspect on the path to formal leadership. An effective leader not only focuses on the challenges and opportunities of the present, but also has a clear idea of where he wants to take his team or his organization in the future. Developing a vision requires a deep understanding of both personal and organizational goals and values. This vision should be inspiring enough to motivate others to follow you and practical enough to be achievable. Communicating this vision clearly and persuasively is what separates a leader who simply manages from one who truly inspires and guides to success. Once you have a clear vision, everything you do as a leader must be aligned with that vision, from daily decisions to long-term strategies.

Another important step on this path is learning to delegate. As a formal leader, you won't be able to do everything yourself. In fact, trying to do it all is not only unsustainable, it can also be detrimental to your team and yourself. Delegating effectively not only frees you to focus on the most important strategic decisions, but also empowers your team, allowing them to develop their own skills and take on more responsibility. Delegating does not simply mean assigning tasks; It means trusting your team, giving them the authority and resources they need to succeed, and being available to support them when they need it. Delegating well requires a clear understanding of each team member's strengths and weaknesses, as well as open and honest communication about expectations and goals.

Resilience is another essential quality on the path to formal leadership. No matter how prepared you are or how many skills you have developed, you will inevitably face challenges, failures, and criticism. Resilience is the ability to bounce back from these setbacks, learn from them, and move forward with even more determination. A resilient leader does not allow himself to be brought down by difficulties, but rather uses them as opportunities to grow and improve. Developing resilience involves cultivating a positive mindset, seeking support when you need it, and maintaining a long-term focus, without losing sight of your goals. Over time, resilience will not only help you meet leadership challenges, but it will also allow you to inspire your team to persevere through difficult times.

Another fundamental aspect of the path to formal leadership is the management of responsibility. As a leader, you will be responsible not only for your own actions, but also for those of your team. This means you will have to make difficult decisions, sometimes under pressure, and take responsibility for the results, whether positive or negative. Handling this responsibility requires integrity, transparency, and a strong work ethic. It is important that you are willing to admit mistakes when you make them and take steps to correct them. At the same time, you must recognize and celebrate successes, both yours and your team's, to maintain motivation and commitment. Responsibility also involves being an example for others, showing through your actions how they should behave and what values should guide their work.

Finally, the path to formal leadership involves a continuous commitment to learning and improvement. Leadership is a constantly evolving field, and what works today may not be effective tomorrow. Therefore, it is crucial that you remain open to learning, always looking for new ways to improve your skills and knowledge. This can include continuing education, reading books and articles on leadership, attending workshops and conferences, and seeking feedback from your peers and team. The willingness to learn and adapt will not only keep you relevant in your leadership role, but will also allow you to lead with confidence in an ever-changing world.

In conclusion, the path to formal leadership is a journey that requires self-awareness, skill development, relationship building, creating a clear vision, ability to delegate, resilience, managing responsibility and a continuous commitment to learning. It is not an easy path, but it is extremely rewarding. Every step you take brings you closer to not only being a formal leader, but to being a leader who inspires, motivates and guides others to success. As you embark on this journey, remember that leadership is more than a title or position; It is a responsibility that you must assume with dedication, integrity and passion. In the end, true leadership success is not measured only by what you accomplish, but by the positive, lasting impact you leave on others.

www.ingramcontent.com/pod-product-compliance
Lightning Source LLC
Chambersburg PA
CBHW031410150726
47989CB00002B/595